This journal belongs to:

_____

Affirmations

I am brave
I am kind
I am beautiful
I am caring
Every day is special
I learn from mistakes
I believe in myself
I value my Family and Friends.

Grateful ≈ Happy

Feeling grateful is proven to increase feelings of happiness. So be like a horse and see the joy in little things.

Food

Sunshine

Kicking up your heels

Friends

Affection and love

Helping others

The outdoors

Respect

Learning new things

Little successes

I am grateful for these moments

Notes

Date	

I am grateful for these moments

Notes

Date	

I am grateful for these moments

Notes

Date	

I am grateful for these moments

Notes

Date	

I am grateful for these moments

Notes

Date	

I am grateful for these moments

Notes

Date

I am grateful for these moments

Notes

Date	

I am grateful for these moments

Notes

Date	

I am grateful for these moments

Notes

Date	

I am grateful for these moments

Notes

Date	

I am grateful for these moments

Notes

Date	

I am grateful for these moments

Notes

Date	

I am grateful for these moments

Notes

Date	

I am grateful for these moments

Notes

Date	

I am grateful for these moments

Notes

Date

I am grateful for these moments

Notes

Date

I am grateful for these moments

Notes

Date	

I am grateful for these moments

Notes

Date

I am grateful for these moments

Notes

Date

I am grateful for these moments

Notes

Date	

I am grateful for these moments

Notes

Date	

I am grateful for these moments

Notes

Date	

I am grateful for these moments

Notes

Date	

I am grateful for these moments

Notes

Date	

I am grateful for these moments

Notes

Date	

I am grateful for these moments

Notes

Date

I am grateful for these moments

Notes

Date

I am grateful for these moments

Notes

Date

I am grateful for these moments

Notes

Date

I am grateful for these moments

Notes

Date	

I am grateful for these moments

Notes

Date

I am grateful for these moments

Notes

Date

I am grateful for these moments

Notes

Date	

I am grateful for these moments

Notes

Date	

I am grateful for these moments

Notes

Date

I am grateful for these moments

Notes

Date

I am grateful for these moments

Notes

Date

I am grateful for these moments

Notes

Date	

I am grateful for these moments

Notes

Date	

I am grateful for these moments

Notes

Date	

I am grateful for these moments

Notes

Date

I am grateful for these moments

Notes

Date	

Manufactured by Amazon.ca
Bolton, ON

35740315R00057